Paragraph Writing

Editorial Development: Marilyn Evans
Jo Ellen Moore
Leslie Sorg
Andrea Weiss
Copy Editing: Cathy Harber
Art Direction: Marcia Smith
Cover Design: Liliana Potigian
Illustration: Don Robison
Design/Production: Jia-Fang Eubanks
Morgan Kashata

EMC 246

Evan-Moor®
EDUCATIONAL PUBLISHERS
Helping Children Learn since 1979

Congratulations on your purchase of some of the finest teaching materials in the world.

Correlated to State Standards

Contents

Paragraph Writing • EMC 246 • © Evan-Moor Corp.

Transparencies

What's Inside

Paragraph Writing provides multiple ways for your students to hone their paragraph writing skills. A wealth of activities on varied difficulty levels allows all students to experience success.

Learning the Parts of the Paragraph

Pages 8–24 contain activities you can use to help your students understand how to identify and write topic sentences and supporting details.

Paragraph Forms

Pages 25–47 contain forms for guiding students to write paragraphs. Students gain experience writing narrative paragraphs, descriptive paragraphs, "how to" paragraphs, and paragraphs that compare and contrast.

Planning Paragraphs Using a Web

Pages 48–53 provide practice using webs to organize information prior to writing paragraphs.

Planning Paragraphs Using an Outline

Pages 54–61 give students practice in using outlines to organize information within paragraphs.

Paragraph Writing Center

The Paragraph Writing Center beginning on page 62 provides writing prompts, open-ended topic sentences, and activities to practice sequencing sentences in paragraphs.

Paragraph Writing Across the Curriculum

The forms and prompts on pages 76–79 provide opportunities for students to practice their writing skills in science, social studies, and math.

Transparencies

This revised edition provides 8 transparencies that make it easier to provide writing models and guide group work.

Trait-Based Writing

Paragraph Writing fits perfectly if you're using trait-based writing! When your students use this book, they develop these skills:

Ideas

- Adding details
- Maintaining focus
- Choosing a specific topic
- Eliminating unnecessary details
- Narrowing your idea for purpose
- Making the topic more interesting
- Making sure details are relevant and interesting
- Writing topic sentences and supporting details

Organization

- Sequencing
- Describing things by position
- Organizing information logically
- Including a beginning, middle, and end
- Organizing information to compare and contrast
- Choosing a structure to match purpose and audience

Conventions

- Indenting paragraphs
- Using commas correctly
- Using correct grammar
- Writing complete sentences
- Beginning each sentence with a capital letter
- Ending each sentence with the correct punctuation

Word Choice

- Writing about action
- Using multiple modifiers
- Using descriptive language
- Getting the reader's attention
- Using strong verbs and adverbs
- Using precise nouns and phrases

Voice

- Developing personal voice
- Distinguishing between different voices
- Using different voices for different purposes
- Choosing words that create a particular mood

Sentence Fluency

- Expanding sentences
- Varying sentence lengths
- Writing complete sentences
- Writing complete paragraphs

Checklist of Skills

Skill	Name												
Identifies supporting details													
Chooses a good topic sentence													
Writes a topic sentence given the supporting details													
Identifies extraneous details													
Writes supporting details given a topic sentence													
Writes descriptive paragraphs													
• guided													
• independently													
Writes narrative paragraphs													
• guided													
• independently													
Writes directions paragraphs													
• guided													
• independently													
Writes compare & contrast paragraphs													
• guided													
• independently													
Uses a web to plan and write a paragraph													
Uses a web to plan and write a multiple-paragraph report													
Uses an outline to plan and write several paragraphs													
Indents the first line of a paragraph													
Uses correct capitalization and punctuation													

Name: _____

Preparing a Paragraph

Mark the box when you have completed the step.

☐ 1. Pick a subject for your paragraph.

☐ 2. Think about the main idea of the paragraph.

☐ 3. Write a topic sentence about the main idea.

☐ 4. Add details to your paragraph.
   Does each detail support the main idea?

☐ 5. Read your paragraph.
   How can you make it better?

☐ 6. Proofread your paragraph.

   • I indented the first word.

   • I used correct punctuation marks.

   • I read my paragraph aloud.

   • It says what I want it to say.

   • I asked a friend to proofread it.

☐ 7. Copy your paragraph in your best handwriting.

☐ 8. Share it with a classmate.

PART I: Parts of a Paragraph

What Is a Paragraph?

Discuss the parts of a paragraph with your students to be sure they understand what a paragraph must contain.

A paragraph must contain a main idea expressed in a topic sentence with additional sentences providing supporting details.

Topic Sentences

Every paragraph should have a main idea expressed in a topic sentence. Provide many experiences in recognizing the main idea of a paragraph and the topic sentence that expresses it. Begin with obvious ones in short paragraphs. Use more complex paragraphs as your students become more proficient.

1 Use pages 9 through 13 for practice identifying topic sentences within paragraphs.

2 Use pages 14 through 17 to practice writing topic sentences.

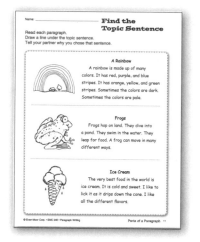

Additional Ideas

• Read sample paragraphs from text or literature books. Help students locate the main ideas and topic sentences.

• Read and display samples from students' own work on transparencies. Have students determine if there is a clear main idea in each and if it is expressed in the topic sentence.

Note: Transparency provided.

What's the Big Idea?

Guided Practice

1. Reproduce pages 9 and 10 or use the transparencies in the back of the book.

2. Have students determine the main idea in each paragraph. You might ask, "What is the most important, or main, idea in this paragraph?"

3. Write the main idea in the space above the paragraph.

4. Then ask, "Which sentence tells you this idea?" Explain that this sentence is called the topic sentence of the paragraph.

5. Underline the topic sentence in each paragraph.

Independent Practice

1. The practice activities on pages 11–13 are scaffolded by degree of difficulty. Select and reproduce the appropriate pages for your students.

2. Have students determine and underline the topic sentences independently.

3. Then have students compare answers with a partner and explain why a sentence was chosen.

4. Check the answers as a class.

Example:

Main Idea: taking care of pet fish

Arnie takes good care of his pet fish. He keeps its bowl filled with fresh water. He feeds it every morning. He keeps his cat away from the bowl. He takes the fish to the vet if it gets sick.

Arnie takes good care of his pet fish. He keeps its bowl filled with fresh water. He feeds it every morning. He keeps his cat away from the bowl. He takes the fish to the vet if it gets sick.

I carry out the trash on Monday morning. I help my dad weed the garden. I make my bed and keep my bedroom tidy. I help my sister with the dinner dishes. Boy, do I have a lot of work to do every week!

Parts of a Paragraph

Maria and Carlos have an unusual job. They perform at birthday parties. Maria plays music on her banjo while Carlos dances. People gather around to watch. They clap their hands and dance with Carlos.

Parts of a Paragraph

As the sun begins to sink below the horizon, the sky starts to change colors. Pink clouds fill the sky, becoming darker as the sun sinks lower. The waves reflect the changing colors as they break along the shore. Sunsets are so beautiful by the sea.

Name: _____

Find the
Topic Sentence

Read each paragraph.
Draw a line under the topic sentence.
Tell your partner why you chose that sentence.

A Rainbow

A rainbow is made up of many colors. It has red, purple, and blue stripes. It has orange, yellow, and green stripes. Sometimes the colors are dark. Sometimes the colors are pale.

Frogs

Frogs hop on land. They dive into a pond. They swim in the water. They leap for food. A frog can move in many different ways.

Ice Cream

The very best food in the world is ice cream. It is cold and sweet. I like to lick it as it drips down the cone. I like all the different flavors.

Find the Topic Sentence

Read each paragraph.
Draw a line under the topic sentence.
Tell your partner why you chose that sentence.

Max's little sister can be a pest. For example, yesterday she drew all over his homework with markers. While he was at school, she messed up the puzzle he had been working on for days. Then at dinner, she knocked her glass of milk over and it landed in his lap.

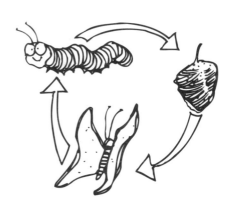

Many changes happen to a caterpillar as it grows. It gets bigger and bigger as it eats leaves. One day, it forms a fuzzy cocoon. After several weeks, a moth crawls out of the cocoon. It flies away once its wings are dry.

When a whale calf is hungry, it bumps its mother. She squirts milk into the calf's mouth. It drinks many gallons of milk in a short time. The milk is so rich that a calf can gain eight pounds (four kilograms) in one hour. A baby whale needs its mother's milk to grow.

Name: _____

Find the
Topic Sentence

Read each paragraph.
Draw a line under the topic sentence.
Tell your partner why you chose that sentence.

Disneyland is an exciting place to visit. First, you can go on many thrilling rides. Second, you can eat all kinds of good food. I like hot dogs and frozen bananas best. Next, there are many shows to see. Finally, you can watch a great parade before you go back home.

Every day at 6 a.m., Kim puts on old clothes and heads for the barn. She takes care of her horse before she goes to school. She carries a bucket of fresh water to his stall. Then, she gets a pail of grain and an armload of alfalfa hay. She puts it in his trough. Finally, she takes him to the pasture where he will graze while she is at school.

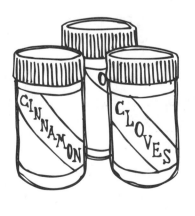

Spices were very valuable in olden times. There was no refrigeration, so foods spoiled more quickly than today. Spices helped preserve food so it would last longer. Spices helped hide the taste of slightly spoiled food. Spices added variety to the taste of food.

What's My Topic Sentence?

Students often write paragraphs that contain many details but no topic sentence. This activity helps students learn how to formulate a topic sentence and to realize that there can be more than one appropriate way to state a paragraph's main idea.

1. Write a set of details from page 15 on the board or use the transparency in the back of the book.

2. Read each detail aloud.

3. Discuss with students what the details have in common.

4. Ask students to think of sentences that describe what the details have in common. Write those sentences on the board or transparency. There are multiple sentences that could describe each set of details.

5. Explain that any of the sentences that describe a set of details could be used as the topic sentence of a paragraph.

6. Have each student select one of the topic sentences suggested by the class and write a paragraph containing the information on the set of details.

7. Encourage students to read aloud their paragraphs.

8. Reproduce pages 16 and 17 for additional practice in selecting and writing topic sentences.

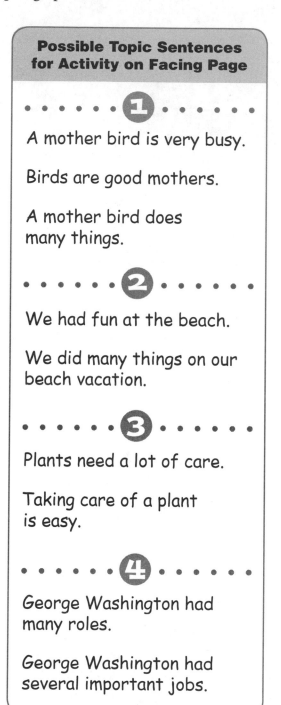

Possible Topic Sentences for Activity on Facing Page

1

A mother bird is very busy.

Birds are good mothers.

A mother bird does many things.

2

We had fun at the beach.

We did many things on our beach vacation.

3

Plants need a lot of care.

Taking care of a plant is easy.

4

George Washington had many roles.

George Washington had several important jobs.

Paragraph Writing • EMC 246 • © Evan-Moor Corp.

1

- build a nest

- lay eggs in the nest

- sit on the eggs

- gather food for the hungry babies

© Evan-Moor Corp. • EMC 246   **Parts of a Paragraph**

2

- built a sand castle

- ran in and out of the waves

- explored the tide pools

- roasted hot dogs over a fire

© Evan-Moor Corp. • EMC 246   **Parts of a Paragraph**

3

- warm sunshine

- water

- fertilizer

- keep free of harmful insects

© Evan-Moor Corp. • EMC 246   **Parts of a Paragraph**

4

- surveyor

- farmer

- general

- first president

© Evan-Moor Corp. • EMC 246   **Parts of a Paragraph**

Name: _____

Best Topic Sentences

Choose the best topic sentence for each set of details. Write it on the line.

Topic Sentences:

Baseball is a good game.

Turtles and snails are a lot alike.

Mom tells me to do this when I get up.

I follow this routine every morning.

This is how to score a home run.

I don't keep my room very clean.

How do you take care of a pet turtle?

Boy, was I surprised when I looked under my bed.

Topic Sentence: _____

Details: wash my face   comb my hair
          brush my teeth   get dressed

Topic Sentence: _____

Details: my lost homework   an old comic book
          a dirty sock   a piece of rotten banana

Topic Sentence: _____

Details: take a bat   hit the ball
          run to home plate   run around all the bases

Topic Sentence: _____

Details: they are animals   they are slow
          they have shells   they eat plants

Name: _____

Write a topic sentence for
each set of details.

Topic Sentence: _____

_____

Details: has no legs   forked tongue
              scaly skin   no eyelids

Topic Sentence: _____

_____

Details: pick it up
              put right arm in right sleeve
              pull it around behind you
              put left arm in left sleeve
              zip it up

Topic Sentence: _____

_____

Details: new shoes   yellow pencils
              a lunchbox   a box of crayons
              school clothes

Supporting Details

The activities in this section provide experiences for students to identify strong supporting details, to eliminate details that don't belong, and to write their own supporting detail sentences.

Identifying Supporting Details

1. Reproduce pages 11–13, previously used to locate topic sentences, for practice identifying sentences that contain supporting details. Have students underline the supporting details in each paragraph.

2. Use pages 19–21 to help students recognize that information that does not support the topic sentence should be excluded from a paragraph. Each of the paragraphs contains a sentence that doesn't belong. Have students identify which sentence should be removed from each paragraph. Use the transparency of page 19 for class practice or to introduce the activities.

Writing Supporting Details

1. Write a topic sentence on the board or overhead projector.

2. List some details under the topic sentence, including at least one detail that does not belong.

3. Read the list with your students.

4. Discuss each detail, asking students if it supports the topic sentence.

5. Cross out any details students agree do not support the topic sentence.

6. Repeat the activity with a new topic sentence.

7. Have students brainstorm ideas that could support it.

8. Write these under the topic sentence.

9. Read the completed list with your students.

10. Discuss each detail, asking students if it supports the topic sentence.

11. Cross out any details students agree do not support the topic sentence.

12. Reproduce pages 22–24 for individual practice in writing supporting details. Have students write three supporting details for each topic sentence.

> Dinosaurs were interesting creatures.
>
> Some were very big.
>
> Some were very small.
>
> They lived a long time ago.
>
> ~~Tyrannosaurus ate meat.~~
>
> Dinosaurs are extinct.

Name: _____

What Doesn't Belong?

Read each paragraph.
Cross out the sentence that doesn't belong.

A New Pet

I would like to have a new pet. I have a cat and a dog. Goldfish and birds would be good pets. Birthdays are fun. Maybe I will get a hamster or a rabbit.

Good Friends

Emily and Tonya are good friends. They play games, ride their bikes, and go to the park together. Tonya's dog can run very fast. Emily and Tonya ride the bus to school together. They spend the night at each other's houses.

Going Swimming

I'm going swimming in the pool at the park. I have my swimsuit and a big towel. Mom gave me money for a snack. Hippos swim in the river. My dad is going to drive me there. It will be a lot of fun.

Name: _____

Read each paragraph.
Cross out the sentence that doesn't belong.

Making Butter

Grandmother showed me how to make butter. First, she got a jar with a lid and some whipping cream. She filled the jar half full of cream. She put the lid on tight. Next, she shook the jar until there were yellow lumps in the liquid. Her dog was taking a nap. Finally, she poured off the liquid and rinsed the butter. Last of all, she spread the butter on hot toast for us to eat. Yummy!

The Water Cycle

Mr. Butler explained the water cycle in science class today. This is how it works. The heat from the sun changes liquid water into water vapor. This is called evaporation. I'm going to play soccer after school today if the sun shines. The water vapor is a gas. The water vapor goes up into the sky. When the water vapor cools, it comes together to make drops. This is condensation. When the drops get heavy, they fall from the sky as rain. This happens over and over again. That is why it is called a "cycle."

     Paragraph Writing • EMC 246 • © Evan-Moor Corp.

Name: _____

What Doesn't Belong?

Read each paragraph.
Cross out the sentence that doesn't belong.

Can I Eat It?

What other people eat may seem strange to you. How would you like a nice juicy grub for a snack? You are probably saying "Yuck!" but in parts of the world, grubs are considered treats. In Sicily, people scoop out the insides of sea urchins for a snack. The French gobble up snails in garlic butter. Did you eat lunch today?

Beavers Build a Home

Beavers build a special home called a lodge. They use trees to build their lodges. Beavers use their sharp teeth to cut down small trees. They cut off the branches and carry the trunks to the stream. Beavers have babies in the spring. They stack the trunks and branches into a big pile. They make the door to the lodge under the water. Beavers are excellent builders.

Name: _____

Write Supporting Details

Read the topic sentence.
Write three supporting details.

Topic Sentence: Pizza is good to eat.

Supporting Details:

1. _____

_____

2. _____

_____

3. _____

_____

Topic Sentence: Elephants are interesting animals.

Supporting Details:

1. _____

_____

2. _____

_____

3. _____

_____

Write Supporting Details

Read the topic sentence.
Write three supporting details.

Topic Sentence: It isn't easy to give a dog a bath.

Supporting Details:

1. _____

_____

2. _____

_____

3. _____

_____

Topic Sentence: It's easy to get from my house to school.

Supporting Details:

1. _____

_____

2. _____

_____

3. _____

_____

Write Supporting Details

Read the topic sentence.
Write three supporting details.

Topic Sentence: I was really scared last night.

Supporting Details:

1. _____

_____

2. _____

_____

3. _____

_____

Topic Sentence: Alex took good care of his brother while Mom
was at the store.

Supporting Details:

1. _____

_____

2. _____

_____

3. _____

_____

PART II: Paragraph Forms

Many students have difficulty writing a paragraph that contains a main idea and supporting details. Establishing forms to follow in the early stages of writing paragraphs will help ensure later success. After students gain proficiency in writing basic paragraphs, move beyond this type of guided practice to "real life" paragraph writing experiences.

The following pages contain sample paragraph forms. You may need to do some as guided lessons with beginning writers. Students with more experience can complete them independently.

Narrative Paragraphs

The paragraphs on pages 27–35 require students to write a paragraph that gives information in a story-like form.

Descriptive Paragraphs

The paragraphs on pages 36–42 require students to describe something. Students must use lively verbs and interesting modifiers to help the reader "see" what they are describing.

"How To" Paragraphs

The paragraphs on pages 43–45 require students to explain how to do something. Some forms use transitional words such as *first*, *second*, *third* or *next*, *then*, and *finally* to help students keep information in a logical order.

Paragraphs That Compare and Contrast

The paragraphs on pages 46 and 47 require students to compare and contrast animals and people.

Using Paragraph Forms

Each paragraph form on pages 27–47 contains two practice activities. The top of each form is a cloze-type activity that provides a guide for the completion of the paragraph. The activity on the bottom of the form provides either a prompt for writing a paragraph on a related topic or a drawing activity.

There are paragraph forms at varying levels of difficulty. Select those most appropriate to your students' writing abilities. If your class is just beginning to write paragraphs, use the forms as guided lessons following the steps below. Progress to independent practice when you feel your students are ready.

As a Guided Lesson

1. Give each child a copy of the form.

2. Brainstorm at each writing point on the form.

   For example, if you were using the form "I'm So Excited" (page 27), you would start by brainstorming ideas with students for the first blank—times when students felt so excited, they would burst. Write these ideas on the board.

   > **exciting times**
   >
   > A on a project
   >
   > new baby brother
   >
   > new puppy

3. Have each student select one idea from the list to copy onto the correct space on the form.

4. Proceed to the next area of the form (whom students ran to tell) and brainstorm a list of people. Again, students select from the list to write a sentence on their forms.

tell	because
mom	she helped me
teacher	he would be excited for me
best friend	our puppies can play together

5. Continue until each writing point of the form has been filled in.

6. Ask students to share their completed paragraphs.

As Independent Practice

1. Give each child a copy of the form.

2. Read the paragraph content and prompts provided. Make sure students understand what to fill in at each writing point.

3. Brainstorm possible words and phrases that might be used. Write these on the board to serve as a reference as students complete their paragraphs.

Name: _____   # Narrative

Complete the paragraph.

I'm So Excited

Have you ever been so excited you felt like you would burst if you didn't tell someone what had happened? I felt that way when

_____

_____

So I ran to tell _____ because _____

_____

_____

_____

Describe a time when you felt lonely. You may follow the pattern above or try to write the paragraph on your own. Remember to use one topic sentence and two or more supporting detail sentences.

_____

_____

_____

_____

_____

Narrative

Complete the paragraph.

What a Miserable Day

Yesterday was the worst day of my life. I felt awful.

It started when _____

_____

Then, _____

_____

_____

The last straw was when _____

_____

Tomorrow has to be better.

Write a paragraph about a time you felt frightened, embarrassed, cheerful, or silly. Explain why you felt that way.

_____

_____

_____

_____

Name: _____ # Narrative

Complete the paragraph.

My Best Friend

Can you guess who my best friend is? She/He _____
(looks like)

_____

She/He can _____
(talents and abilities)

_____

_____

I can always count on her/him to _____

If you guessed _____ , you are right!

Who is your hero? Write a topic sentence and three supporting details explaining why this person is your hero.

_____

_____

_____

_____

_____

Name: _____ # Narrative

Complete the paragraph.

Dinosaurs

In my opinion, the most unusual dinosaur was _____

_____

(Give three or more reasons.)

_____

_____

_____

_____

_____

Write another paragraph about any animal—living, extinct, or imaginary.

_____

_____

_____

_____

_____

_____

Name: _____ # Narrative

Complete the paragraph.

Party Time

My friend's _____ party was the most

fun I've ever had. Everyone had to _____

Then, we _____

Best of all was when _____

_____

I didn't want the party to end!

Write about the worst party you ever attended.

_____

_____

_____

_____

_____

_____

Narrative

Complete the paragraph.

Spiders in the Bedroom

Herman saw a spider crawling across the ceiling of his

bedroom. It was _____

_____

Herman felt _____

_____

He decided _____

_____

_____

In the first box, draw the spider.
In the second box, draw Herman's face when he saw the spider.
In the third box, show what Herman decided to do.

Name: _____ **Narrative**

Complete the paragraph.

The Mysterious _____

    Kelly found an unusual _____ on the

way home from school. When she started to rub the dirt off

the _____,

strange things began to happen. First, she noticed _____

_____ Then, _____

But the strangest thing was when _____

_____

Continue the story about Kelly and her unusual _____.

_____

_____

_____

_____

_____

_____

Narrative

Complete the paragraph.

Planet X

When the first spaceship landed on Planet X, the astronauts were not prepared for what they found. As soon as they

stepped off the ship, they noticed _____

_____

Then, they_____

_____

The most exciting discovery was _____

_____

Illustrate Planet X. Show what the astronauts found there.

Name: _____ # Narrative

Complete the paragraph.

Uncle Moe's Present

Uncle Moe sent me a present for my birthday. It was the

worst present I had ever received. _____

_____

_____

_____

_____

_____

Tell about the best present you ever received.
What was it? Who gave it to you? Why was it the best present?

_____

_____

_____

_____

_____

_____

Name: _____

Descriptive

Complete the paragraph.

Lunchtime

I hate to find _____ in my lunch.

_____

(Describe how it looks.)

_____

_____

(Describe how it tastes.)

_____

_____

It makes me want to _____

Write another paragraph about what you hate to find on the breakfast table. Follow the same pattern you just practiced. Underline your topic sentence.

_____

_____

_____

_____

_____

Paragraph Writing • EMC 246 • © Evan-Moor Corp.

Descriptive

Complete the paragraph.

Let's Eat

The very best food in the world is _____

_____

(Describe how it looks.)

_____

(Describe how it smells.)

_____

(Describe how it tastes.)

_____

_____

You should try it some time. I bet you will like it, too.

Write a paragraph about your favorite dessert or snack. Describe how it looks, smells, and tastes. Explain why you think someone else should try it.

_____

_____

_____

_____

_____

Descriptive

Complete the paragraph.

What a Noise

Pet stores are very noisy places. _____

(Give three examples of how noisy they are.)

_____

_____

_____

_____

The next time I go to one, I will _____

_____

Write about a quiet place. Give three reasons it is quiet.

_____

_____

_____

_____

_____

_____

Descriptive

Complete the paragraph.

Unusual Places

If you could see under my bed, you would be amazed! The

first thing you would notice is _____

_____

Next, _____

_____

Finally, _____

_____

Now, tell me what it's like under your bed.

Write about another unusual place someone could look. Follow the same pattern you just practiced. Underline your supporting sentences.

_____

_____

_____

_____

Descriptive

Complete the paragraph.

By the Sea

Picnics at the beach are really fun, but you do have to plan

carefully. This is what I do. First, I see if _____

(how you will get to the beach)

_____

Then, I invite _____

_____

Finally, I pack a lunch of _____

_____

By the way, don't forget to read the weather report! Have fun.

Explain what you would do if it started to rain after you got to the beach.

_____

_____

_____

_____

_____

_____

Paragraph Writing • EMC 246 • © Evan-Moor Corp.

Descriptive

Complete the paragraph.

Monkey Snack

Last week at the zoo, I saw a monkey eat a banana. This is

what it did. First, _____

Then, _____

Finally, it _____

_____

_____

Maybe I'll eat one myself!

Pretend you are going to eat a slice of watermelon. Write a topic sentence. Give at least three steps telling what you will do.

_____

_____

_____

_____

_____

_____

Name: _____

Descriptive

Complete the paragraph.

Frogs

Frogs are very interesting animals. I like the way they look.

_____

(Tell about how they look.)

_____

Frogs can move in several ways. _____

(Tell ways they move.)

_____

_____

The most interesting fact about frogs is _____

_____

_____

Illustrate one of your paragraphs.

Paragraph Writing • EMC 246 • © Evan-Moor Corp.

Name: _____ # Directions

Complete the paragraph.

How to Fix a Sandwich

I like to fix my own sandwiches. Sometimes I make myself a

_____ sandwich. First, I _____

_____

Second, I _____

Third, I _____

Last of all, I _____

It tastes great with a large glass of _____ to drink.

Draw a picture in each box to show the steps you followed to make a sandwich.

First

Second

Third

Last

Directions

Complete the paragraph.

Bath Time

You may think it is easy to give a pet a bath. Not when it's

a _____ First, you have to _____

_____

Next, you _____

Then, you _____

Finally, you _____

_____ Now you need to take a bath yourself!

Pretend you have to feed applesauce to a baby. Give at least three steps you have to follow.

_____

_____

_____

_____

_____

Directions

Complete the paragraph.

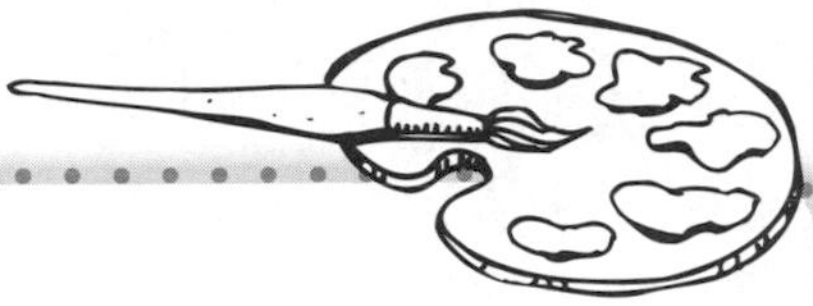

Artist at Work

There are certain steps you must follow when you want to

paint a picture. First, you must get _____

Second, you _____

Next, you _____

_____

Last, _____

_____

_____

Think of a project you would like to make. List the steps you have to follow.

_____

_____

_____

_____

_____

Name: _____

Compare and Contrast

Complete the paragraph.

Bats and Birds

Bats and birds are alike in several ways. They both _____

They also _____

_____

Finally, _____

_____

_____

You can probably think of more ways they are the same.

Now write a paragraph that explains how bats and birds are different.

_____

_____

_____

_____

_____

   Paragraph Writing • EMC 246 • © Evan-Moor Corp.

Name: _____

Compare and Contrast

Complete the paragraph.

The First and Sixteenth Presidents

Although George Washington and Abraham Lincoln were both presidents of the United States, their lives were very different.

_____

_____

_____

I think the biggest difference was _____

_____

Write two or more supporting sentences.

Although George Washington and Abraham Lincoln lived at different times, their lives were similar in many ways.

_____

_____

_____

_____

PART III: Planning Paragraphs Using a Web

Students who are just beginning to write paragraphs or are unfamiliar with webs will need to begin with the simple one-section web described below. More experienced writers can use multisection webs to write a report or story with more than one paragraph. (See pages 51–53.)

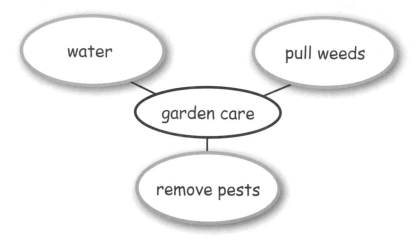

1. Draw the above web on the board.

2. Explain what each circle contains. (center—main idea; outside circles—supporting details) Tell students you will use the web to write a paragraph using the information in the circles.

3. Point to the main idea in the center circle. Work as a class to develop possible topic sentences. Write those sentences on the board.

Sample topic sentences:

> Taking care of a garden is a lot of work.
>
> There are several steps in taking care of a garden.

4. With each supporting detail, point to the circle and discuss ways to write a sentence for that detail. Write these on the board.

Sample supporting sentences:

> Be sure to water your garden often. Pull weeds so the plants can grow. Remove any pests that will harm the plants.

5. Distribute sheets of paper. Have students select one main idea sentence to write as the first sentence of their paragraph. (Remind them to indent.) Then have students choose one sentence for each supporting detail to complete their paragraphs. Ask students to share their completed paragraphs.

6. Reproduce the facing page for practice completing a web and page 50 for writing from a web.

Complete the Web

Read the topic sentences.
Add supporting details.

I help at home.

Clowns are fun
to watch.

Name: _____

Write a Paragraph

Read the information on the web.
Write a paragraph about "fun at the beach."

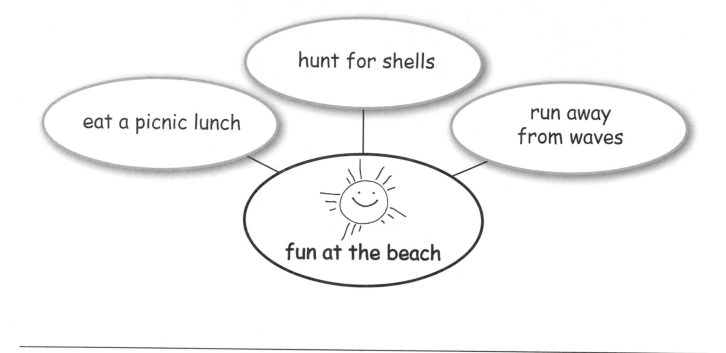

_____

_____

_____

_____

_____

_____

_____

_____

Paragraph Writing • EMC 246 • © Evan-Moor Corp.

Using a Multisection Web

Introduction to a Multisection Web

1. Reproduce page 52 or use the transparency in the back of the book.

2. Tell students that they will often write more than one paragraph about a topic. Each paragraph must have a main idea and details.

3. Show students the completed multisection web on page 52. Point out that "My Pet Dog" is the subject. Have students read each main idea and its supporting details.

4. Then explain how each section of the web becomes a separate paragraph. Point out the separate sections to students.

Setting Up a Web

Reproduce or use the transparency of the blank web on page 53, or draw a web on the board. Guide students through the following steps to complete the web. Fill in the circles as they contribute answers.

1. Select a subject and write it in the large center oval.

2. Think of two or more important things you want to say about the subject. Write these ideas in the ovals stemming from the center oval. These are the main ideas for each paragraph.

   This is a difficult step for many students. Spend some time discussing the types of ideas they come up with. Is the idea really a main idea? Or is it a supporting detail for a main idea?

3. Write supporting details in the ovals stemming from the main idea ovals.

are funny · help students · teachers · work hard · our school · new gym · students · buildings · are kind · big library

Writing from a Web

Distribute writing paper. Using the web you created as a class, work with one section at a time to create paragraphs. You may wish to write the composition over more than one writing session.

1. Ask, "What would be a good topic sentence using the first main idea?"

2. Write students' suggestions on the board. When you have a list, select one, and have students copy it onto their papers.

3. Have students use the supporting details to write three sentences describing the main idea.

4. Repeat the process with the remaining two sections of the web.

Multisection Webs

A web can contain many sections, with each section setting up the main idea and supporting ideas for a paragraph.

Note: Transparency provided.

Name: _____

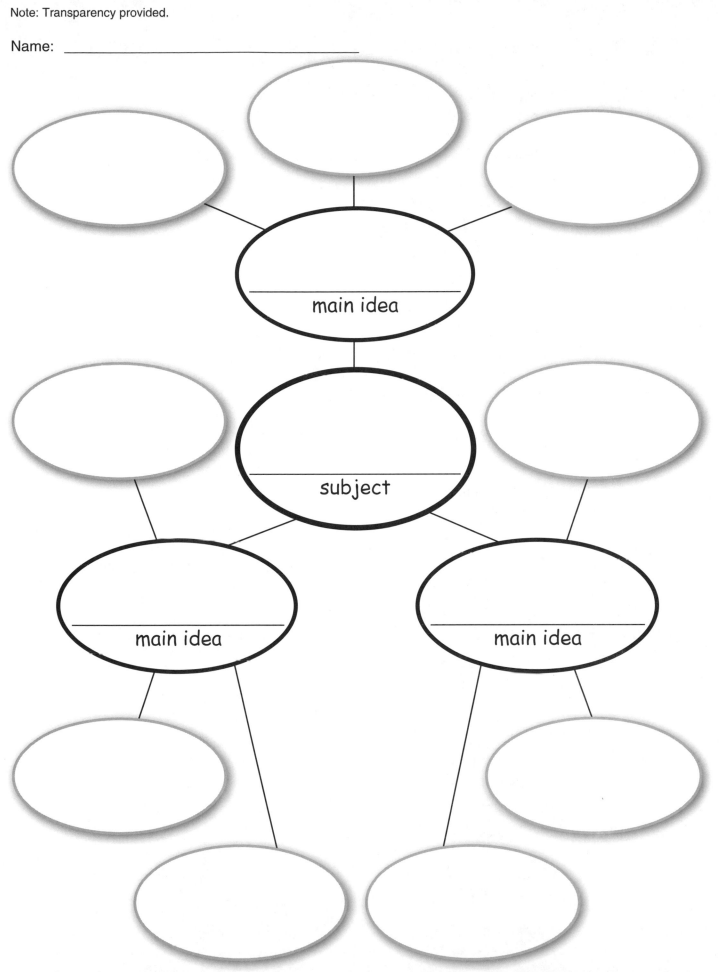

main idea

subject

main idea

main idea

PART IV: Planning Paragraphs Using an Outline

Outlining is another organizational method older or more advanced writers can use when they are writing a composition requiring more than one paragraph.

Introducing an Outline

1. Display the transparency of page 55. Identify it as an outline. Explain that an outline is a way to organize information.

2. Inform students that an outline uses a specific format.

   • Roman numerals indicate main ideas. (Review Roman numerals if necessary.)

   • Capital letters indicate supporting details.

3. Guide students to understand that each section of the outline will become one paragraph of the composition.

4. Using the transparency, complete the outline by filling in information next to the labels.

   • Choose a subject that students are familiar with, such as a local celebration.

   • Have students suggest main ideas and supporting details.

   • Fill in the information on the transparency.

Completing an Outline

1. Reproduce page 56 for each student or use the transparency in the back of the book.

2. Display the transparency and discuss the topic and main ideas shown on the outline.

3. Have students suggest a game to use for the outline. Work as a group to fill in the supporting details.

   Have students copy the topic and details onto their papers. Save their papers.

4. Reproduce page 57 for additional practice in filling in supporting details.

Writing from an Outline

As a group:

1. Use the outline developed on page 56 to create paragraphs. Ask, "What would be a good topic sentence using the first main idea?" Write students' suggestions on the board. When you have a list, select one and have students copy it onto their papers.

2. Have students use the supporting details to suggest three sentences describing the equipment you need. Write these sentences on the board and have students copy them.

3. Repeat the process with the remaining two sections of the outline. You may wish to complete this lesson over several writing blocks.

Individually:

Reproduce pages 58 and 59 for additional practice in writing from a completed outline. Students may need the additional writing paper on page 60.

Making Independent Outlines

Page 61 provides a blank form to use when your students are ready to write outlines independently.

Note: Transparency provided.

Subject of the Report

I. Main Idea

A. supporting detail

B. supporting detail

C. supporting detail

II. Main Idea

A. supporting detail

B. supporting detail

C. supporting detail

III. Main Idea

A. supporting detail

B. supporting detail

C. supporting detail

Name: _____

How to Play _____
(name of game)

I. Equipment you need

A. _____

B. _____

C. _____

II. How to play the game

A. _____

B. _____

C. _____

III. How to keep score

A. _____

B. _____

C. _____

Name: ______________________________

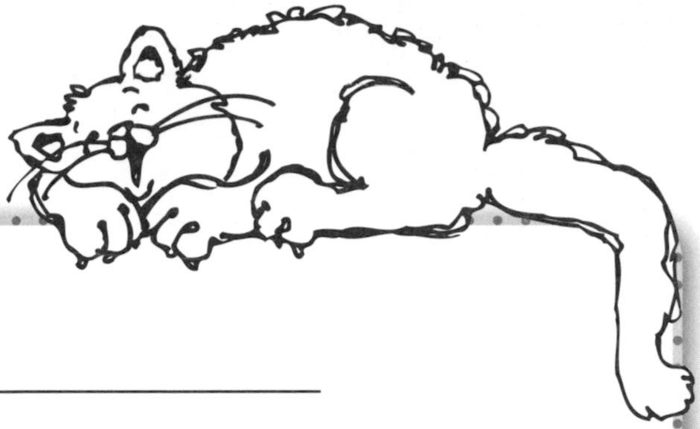

My Pet ____________________

I. What my pet looks like

A. ______________________________

B. ______________________________

C. ______________________________

II. What my pet can do

A. ______________________________

B. ______________________________

C. ______________________________

III. How I take care of my pet

A. ______________________________

B. ______________________________

C. ______________________________

Name: _____

Write a Paragraph

Use this outline.
Write two paragraphs about mother birds.

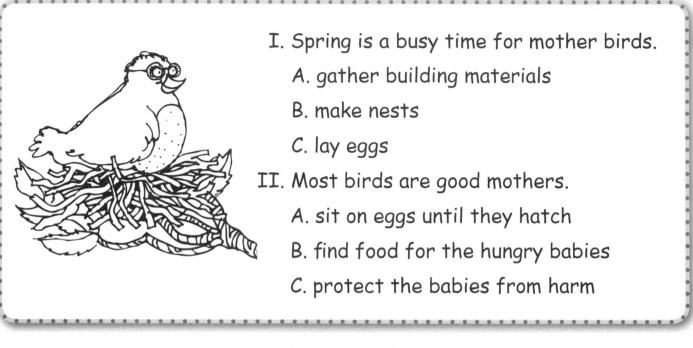

I. Spring is a busy time for mother birds.
  A. gather building materials
  B. make nests
  C. lay eggs
II. Most birds are good mothers.
  A. sit on eggs until they hatch
  B. find food for the hungry babies
  C. protect the babies from harm

Mother Birds

_____

_____

_____

_____

_____

_____

_____

_____

     Paragraph Writing • EMC 246 • © Evan-Moor Corp.

Name: _____

Write a Paragraph

Use this outline.
Write two paragraphs about having a pizza party.

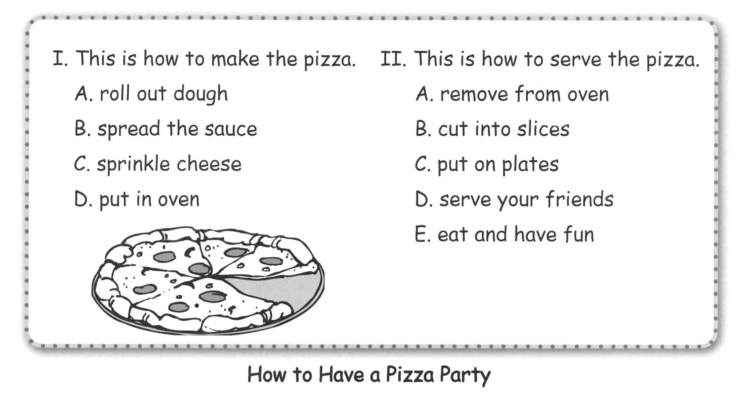

I. This is how to make the pizza.

    A. roll out dough

    B. spread the sauce

    C. sprinkle cheese

    D. put in oven

II. This is how to serve the pizza.

    A. remove from oven

    B. cut into slices

    C. put on plates

    D. serve your friends

    E. eat and have fun

How to Have a Pizza Party

_____

_____

_____

_____

_____

_____

Planning Paragraphs Using an Outline

Name: _____

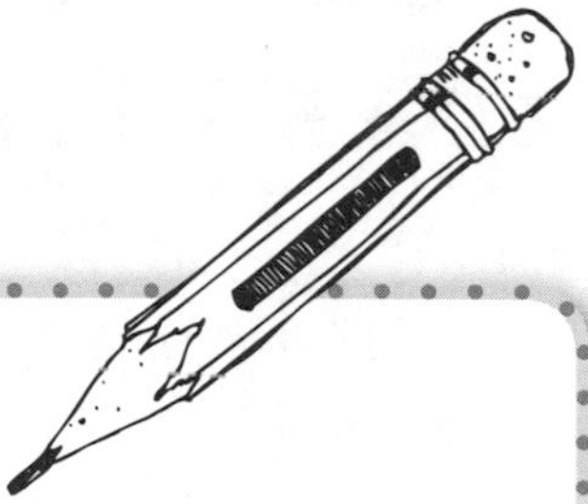

_____
(subject)

I. _____

   A. _____

   B. _____

   C. _____

II. _____

   A. _____

   B. _____

   C. _____

III. _____

   A. _____

   B. _____

   C. _____

PART V: Paragraph Writing Center

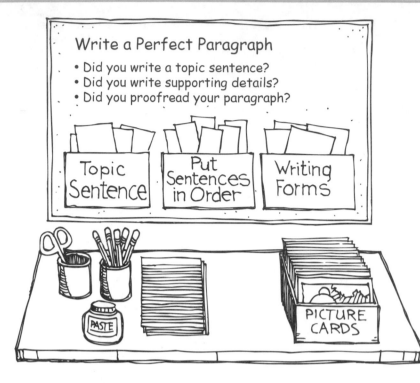

Write a Perfect Paragraph
• Did you write a topic sentence?
• Did you write supporting details?
• Did you proofread your paragraph?

Topic Sentence

Put Sentences in Order

Writing Forms

PICTURE CARDS

PASTE

Supplies:

• writing and drawing paper
• pencils and erasers
• pushpins

Activities

Put Sentences in Order

1. Prepare the sentence strips and answer keys. Reproduce pages 63–66.

   • Glue the sentences for each paragraph to a different color of construction paper, laminate, and cut apart. Place the sentences for each paragraph in a separate envelope.

   • Reproduce the answer keys on pages 67 and 68. Glue or staple each answer onto construction paper. Place each answer in the envelope with the correct sentence strips.

2. Students place the strips in an order that makes sense and then look at the answer key to see if they are correct.

Writing Forms

Provide copies of any of the paragraph forms on pages 27–47.

Picture Cards

1. Reproduce several copies of the picture cards on pages 69–72.

2. Cut the cards apart and place each picture set in a separate envelope. Glue one picture on the front of the envelope to indicate the envelope's contents.

3. Students choose a picture, attach it to a sheet of writing paper, and write one or more paragraphs.

Topic Sentences

Prepare the open-ended topic sentences on pages 73–75 to use as starters for paragraph writing. Glue the sentences to construction paper, laminate, and cut apart. Place these in a can or box at the writing center.

Plug in the toaster.

Add butter.

Put the bread into the slots.

Then eat!

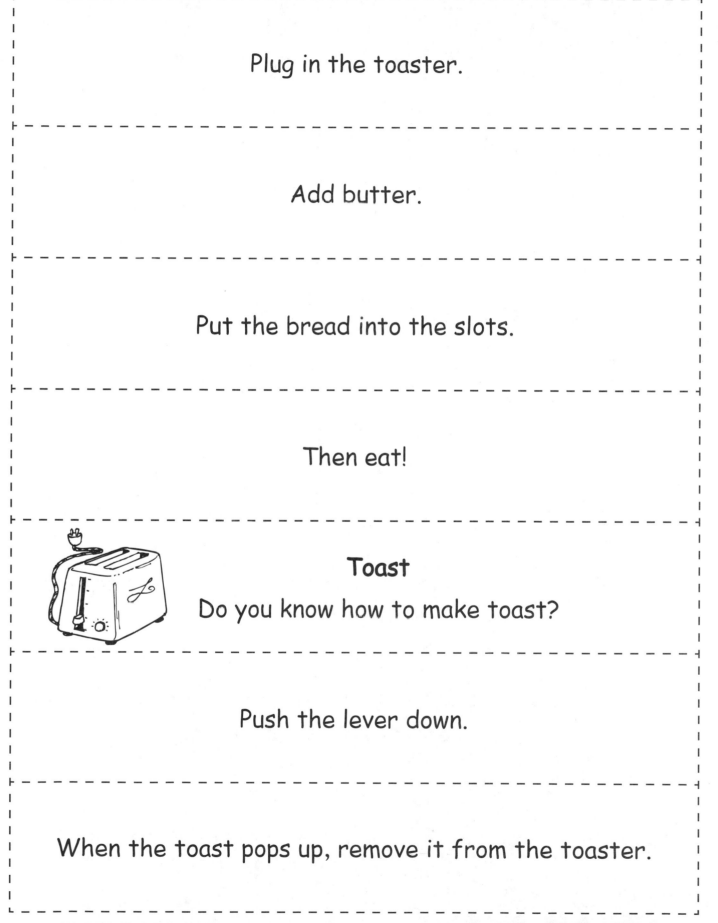

Toast

Do you know how to make toast?

Push the lever down.

When the toast pops up, remove it from the toaster.

She lays eggs in the nest and covers them up.

A mother alligator builds a nest of plants and mud.

The baby alligators make a noise when they hatch.

Alligator Mother

An alligator is a good mother.

She takes good care of her new babies after they hatch.

When she hears the noise, she digs open
the nest so the babies can get out.

     Paragraph Writing • EMC 246 • © Evan-Moor Corp.

She had to wait until she started school.

Kristi began dancing lessons and tumbling classes when she was only four.

So when Kristi began first grade, she also began ice-skating lessons.

Kristi Yamaguchi

Kristi Yamaguchi started early and worked hard to become an Olympic skating champion.

Kristi wanted to take skating lessons, too.

These tiny, tiny plants are eaten by
tiny animals (copepods).

Tiny, tiny plants (diatoms) in the sea get
their energy from the sun.

A person catches the large fish and eats it.

The small fish are eaten by large fish.

Food Chain

If you ever eat fish, you are part of
a food chain that begins with the sun.

The tiny animals are eaten by small fish.

That person gets energy from the fish when it is eaten.

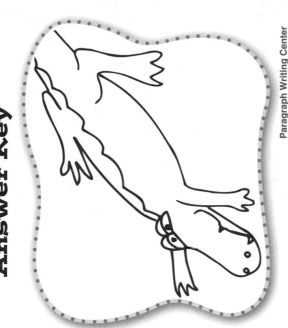

Alligator Mother

An alligator is a good mother. A mother alligator builds a nest of plants and mud. She lays eggs in the nest and covers them up. The baby alligators make a noise when they hatch. When she hears the noise, she digs open the nest so the babies can get out. She takes good care of her new babies after they hatch.

Toast

Do you know how to make toast? Plug in the toaster. Put the bread into the slots. Push the lever down. When the toast pops up, remove it from the toaster. Add butter. Then eat!

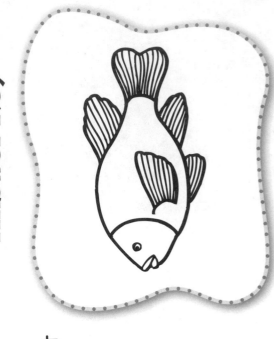

Kristi Yamaguchi

Kristi Yamaguchi started early and worked hard to become an Olympic skating champion. Kristi began dancing lessons and tumbling classes when she was only four. Kristi wanted to take skating lessons, too. She had to wait until she started school. So when Kristi began first grade, she also began ice-skating lessons.

Food Chain

If you ever eat fish, you are part of a food chain that begins with the sun. Tiny, tiny plants (diatoms) in the sea get their energy from the sun. These tiny, tiny plants are eaten by tiny animals (copepods). The tiny animals are eaten by small fish. The small fish are eaten by large fish. A person catches the large fish and eats it. That person gets energy from the fish when it is eaten.

Picture Cards

Describe:

Tell how to make:

Tell how to play:

Compare:

Paragraph Writing Center

Paragraph Writing Center

Paragraph Writing Center

Paragraph Writing Center

Describe:

Paragraph Writing Center

Tell how to fix:

Paragraph Writing Center

Describe:

Paragraph Writing Center

Compare:

Paragraph Writing Center

Paragraph Writing • EMC 246 • © Evan-Moor Corp.

Describe:

© Evan-Moor Corp. • EMC 246   **Paragraph Writing Center**

Tell how to clean:

© Evan-Moor Corp. • EMC 246   **Paragraph Writing Center**

Tell how to take care of:

© Evan-Moor Corp. • EMC 246   **Paragraph Writing Center**

Compare:

© Evan-Moor Corp. • EMC 246   **Paragraph Writing Center**

Tell how he feels:

© Evan-Moor Corp. • EMC 246   **Paragraph Writing Center**

Describe:

© Evan-Moor Corp. • EMC 246   **Paragraph Writing Center**

Contrast:

© Evan-Moor Corp. • EMC 246   **Paragraph Writing Center**

Tell how to plant a garden:

GARDEN SOIL

SEEDS
SEEDS

© Evan-Moor Corp. • EMC 246   **Paragraph Writing Center**

Topic Sentence	Topic Sentence	Topic Sentence	Topic Sentence
I love to eat _____ more than anything else in the world.	I saw something strange on the way to school today.	Rain makes me feel _____ for many reasons.	I just read a good book about _____. I learned...

Topic Sentence	Topic Sentence	Topic Sentence	Topic Sentence
I have really changed since I was six. Then... Now...	The worst book I ever read was _____. I didn't like it for these reasons:	I know how to fix a broken _____. First, ...	_____ have important jobs. They...

Topic Sentence	**Topic Sentence**	**Topic Sentence**	**Topic Sentence**
This is how to play ———— .	I had trouble sleeping last night.	I'll never forget the first time I ever saw a ———— .	Did you ever notice how much ———— and ———— are alike?

PART VI: Paragraph Writing Across the Curriculum

Once your students have had some experience writing paragraphs, provide opportunities to practice throughout the day. With a little creativity and planning, you can incorporate paragraph writing into curriculum areas. Pages 77–79 provide forms for students to practice writing paragraphs in science, social studies, and math.

Here are other suggestions for writing across the curriculum:

	Science	Social Studies	Math
Narrative	• Explain what a scientist does. • Explain how magnets work.	• Retell an event from history. • Tell how a person might have felt during some historic event (war, plague, trip across desert or plains, immigration).	• Rewrite an equation in paragraph form. • Tell how charts are used in math.
Descriptive	• Describe what was seen during an observation. • Describe the life cycle of an animal or insect.	• Describe the clothing people wore in another time period. • Describe the country you would most like to visit.	• Describe the differences between a circle and a triangle. • Describe your feelings when doing math.
Directions	• Explain how to conduct an experiment. • Explain how to recycle in your home. • Explain how to measure something.	• Explain how to make something used in a different time period. • Give directions to Oregon from Independence, Missouri, following the Oregon Trail.	• Explain how to solve a math problem. • Explain how to cut eight equal slices of pizza.
Compare and Contrast	• Compare two animals, objects, or procedures. • Compare or contrast two habitats. • Contrast a desert and a forest.	• Compare and contrast two people, events, time periods, etc. • Compare your life to that of a person your age in another country or time period.	• Compare a rectangle and a square. • Compare and contrast addition and subtraction.

Write a Science Paragraph

Watch an animal. Tell what you see.

This is what the _____ looked like.
(animal)

_____

_____

_____

_____

_____

_____

This is what the _____ did as I watched.
(animal)

_____

_____

_____

_____

_____

_____

Write a Social Studies Paragraph

Imagine that you lived during the time of _____.

Describe what you wore.

_____

_____

_____

_____

_____

Describe where you lived.

_____

_____

_____

_____

_____

Write a Math Paragraph

Tell how a square and a triangle are different.

_____

_____

_____

_____

_____

Rewrite this number sentence as a paragraph:

9 crows + 3 woodpeckers = 12 birds

_____

_____

_____

_____

_____